Worship Resources
For
Special Sundays

Stan Purdum
Pamela J. Abbey
Elaine M. Ward

CSS Publishing Company, Inc., Lima, Ohio

WORSHIP RESOURCES FOR SPECIAL SUNDAYS

For more information about CSS Publishing Company resources, visit our website at
www.csspub.com or e-mail us at custserv@csspub.com or call (800) 241-4056.

ISBN 0-7880-1974-0   PRINTED IN U.S.A.

Foreword

The church calendar is filled with many special Sundays and events. In September, church and Sunday school activities return to full schedules, beginning with Rally Day events and worship. October brings Reformation Day, followed by All Saints' Day and Thanksgiving in November. Hard on the heels of Thanksgiving come the special Sundays in Advent and preparing for the celebration of our Savior's birth. And sometime in the winter months, we take the opportunity to uplift our youth and encourage them in their worship skills.

This collection includes worship resources, written by three authors, for these special events in the church year:

Stan Purdum has provided worship services and sermons for Rally Day, Reformation Sunday, All Saints' Sunday, and Thanksgiving.

Pamela J. Abbey has written four monologues for the Sundays in Advent to help prepare the congregation for the celebration of the coming of the Lord. Joseph, Cousin Jochaved, a Shepherd, and an Angel speak.

Elaine M. Ward has created a Youth Sunday worship service and accompanying children's message.

Table Of Contents

Service Of Worship

Rally Day

Welcome and Announcements

Prelude

Call to Worship
One: Go, make of all disciples.
All: We hear the call, O Lord.
One: It comes from our Creator.
All: The Bible tells us so.
One: Let us cultivate learning;
All: Let us teach the Holy Word.
One: Revealing in our witness
All: The master teacher's art.
　　　　— adapted from the hymn, "Go, Make Of All Disciples"
　　　　(Leon M. Adkins)

*Hymn　　　　　　　　　　　　"All Things Bright And Beautiful"

*Invocation
　　Let this service of worship, O God, be a channel by which you speak to us afresh. Enable us to listen carefully, praise joyfully, and respond wholeheartedly. Amen.

*Praise Chorus　　　　　　　　　　　　　"Holy Ground"

Responsive Scripture　　　　　　　　　Colossians 3:12-17

Children's Moments

Sunday School Choruses

"Deep And Wide"
"Peace Like A River"
"Hallelujah!"
"I've Got The Joy, Joy, Joy, Joy"

Presentation of Tithes and Offerings

Offertory
*Doxology

Morning Prayer

O God of life and learning, you have committed to our care developing Christians, children and adults. You have entrusted us with the scriptures, and the message of your justice, grace, power, and love. Shine your wisdom upon us so that those who teach and those who learn may grow in faith and understanding through the ministry of our Sunday school.

Help us who teach, that in our teaching, we will steadfastly pass the faith along from person to person, so that each new generation might have the opportunity to learn about you and to accept Jesus Christ for themselves.

Help us who learn, that in our learning, we may receive not only knowledge for the Christian journey, but the presence of Jesus himself.

In his name we pray. Amen.

Scripture   Mark 10:1, 13-16

Sermon   The Saga Of Bobby Wildgoose

Commissioning our Sunday School Teachers
[Use service from denominational worship book]

*Hymn   "Jesus Loves Me"

*Benediction

*Postlude

The Saga Of Bobby Wildgoose

Mark 10:1, 13-16

The year was 1780. The place, Gloucester, England. It was a growing town, but not a particularly happy one. It was becoming an industrial center, but the unregulated rapid growth that accompanied the influx of industry exacted a high price from the community. Crime was on the rise, the poor were being exploited, and sanitary conditions were terrible. Open sewers ran along the sides of the streets.

Even worse, those were the days before child labor laws and free public education. Most children from the lower classes worked twelve-hour days, six days a week in the factories. On Sundays, their only day off, most of these kids simply ran the streets, playing games of chance, watching cock fights, stealing, and generally getting into mischief.

It happened that one day, a newspaperman by the name of Robert Raikes had to visit the local jail to see one of his employees who had landed there for some offense. In the course of that visit, Raikes was shocked to discover that all manner of people were confined there together. People of both sexes and all ages were housed in filthy conditions. Children, arrested for stealing a piece of fruit, were in the same cells with convicted adult felons. Raikes, a man with a sense of social responsibility, talked to some of these wretched prisoners and learned that one of the chief reasons for their getting involved in crime was ignorance of any other way of life.

After that visit, Raikes tried to help some of these individuals reform, but he soon found that people were entering the prison system faster than he could help them.

Some time later, a business errand took Raikes to a rundown part of the city known as Sooty Alley. There he observed a number

9

of ragged children, cursing a blue streak and running uncared for. A woman of the neighborhood told Raikes that since that was a weekday, most of the area's children were in the factories. But come Sunday, she said, the streets would be filled with filthy urchins getting into all kinds of trouble. As far as she was concerned, she said, the sooner the kids found their way into jail, the better.

It struck Raikes, however, that if something could be done to help the young, to get them on the right track, then perhaps the stream of humanity flooding the prisons could be stemmed. Ah, he thought, a nice idea, but what could one man do in the face of such overwhelming odds?

At that moment, he heard a voice inside him say, "Try." "But I am only one person," he protested. Again the inner voice said, "Try."

He thought about that disturbing command briefly, and before the day was over, he went out and, out of his own pocket, hired four women to teach as many children as he could round up the next Sunday. When that day came, Raikes returned to Sooty Alley and got a large number of curious children to follow him to the place he'd arranged for this endeavor. There, Raikes, along with the four women, began instructing the kids in reading and in the church catechism.

And so it continued each Sunday. The children of Gloucester came to love Robert Raikes. He was a chubby man with a round, friendly face, and he wore a snow-white wig. Partly because of his appearance and partly because of his bustling energy, the children nicknamed him Bobby Wildgoose.

Guess what? That was the beginning of the Sunday School movement. Of course, the first Sunday schools were much differ-ent than ours. They were Christian schools, but because the kids involved didn't go to public school, Raikes and his teachers had to teach the whole gamut — the three R's plus hygiene and reli-gion. The school lasted for several hours each Sunday and in-cluded a break to attend worship at a nearby church. Raikes was tireless in recruiting children for his school, and all that he re-quired for admission was cleanliness, good behavior, and respect for the teachers.

Raikes paid those first teachers a shilling a week, but as Sunday schools spread to other towns, the practice of paying teachers soon ended. Only five years after the first Sunday school began, a Sunday school teacher in Oldham, England, refused his weekly stipend and insisted on teaching as a volunteer instead. This, in turn, made Sunday schools more self-supporting and less dependent on the wealthy class for support.

Before long, Sunday schools were springing up in many places. In 1785, they jumped the Atlantic and came to America. By 1810, only thirty years after Raikes' answered God's call to "try," the movement included more than 3,000 schools with a combined enrollment of 275,000 pupils. And of course Sunday schools have grown far beyond that today. In Wales, as early as 1811, separate classes for adults were added to Sunday schools, and this soon became a common practice throughout the Sunday school movement.

The poor were the immediate beneficiaries of Sunday schools. For most of them, the Sunday school was their only means of instruction. In time, with the advent of public education, Sunday schools were able to concentrate solely on religious instruction, but even by then, Sunday schools were responsible for shaping the faith and morals of several generations, as well as imparting Bible knowledge.

In the scripture reading for today, Jesus was teaching a crowd. (In fact, "Teacher" or "Rabbi," which means the same thing, was one of the more common titles by which Jesus was addressed.) Some people wanted to bring their children to Jesus for him to touch them, but the disciples tried to stop them. But Jesus made it clear they were to be allowed to come to him, "for it is to such as these that the kingdom of God belongs."

But Jesus went on to sweep us all in: "Whoever does not receive the kingdom of God as a little child will never enter it."

Surely Raikes, in working with children, was doing his part to bring children the opportunity to enter God's kingdom. But imagine what would have been lost if, when he heard the voice saying, "Try," he had answered, "I can't."

I can imagine that not everyone teaching Sunday school across America feels up to the job. But time and again, people hear the call to try, and with God's help, become a positive influence on other people's lives.

Two teenagers grew up in Dallas. Both were rough and troublesome. But a faithful Sunday school teacher contacted one of them every Sunday for a year. Another teacher was urged to invite the second boy but the teacher felt he didn't want that kind of trouble in his class. The first teen finally responded. He grew up to become the Secretary of Evangelism for the Baptist Church in Florida. The other boy grew up and assassinated President John F. Kennedy. We cannot say for certain that Sunday school would have prevented that, but it might have.

You know that during the week I work in the business world. I came to that position after 25 years of being full-time in the church. Coming from that background, one of the things I've learned to really appreciate about business is how quickly things can get done. The church does many things well, but being quickly responsive to fixing things is not one of them.

I hate to admit this about church structures, but one of the things that drove me crazy, especially on the conference level, was that when we saw a problem that needed to be improved or fixed, instead of trying something, we organized a committee. That committee would meet; every faction's ideas and complaints were listened to and hashed over and then finally some recommendations were made. That report would go to annual conference where it would be debated, amended, and finally voted on. If it passed, a new committee would be assigned to implement it. A couple of years after the start, something might actually happen.

In business, we might discuss a problem for a day or two, but then we formulate a plan and start implementing it within the week. I've seen completely new products come to market just three months after being conceived.

Now I recognize that churches and businesses are different sorts of institutions, but I do think there are lessons that each can learn from the other. In many cases, businesses need to learn compassion from the church. But the church needs to learn *a bias for action* from business. In a comparison study done a few years ago of businesses that succeeded with businesses that weren't doing well, researchers came to this conclusion. The main difference between the two was that the failing businesses spent too much time and energy on planning, trying to cover every possible eventuality before moving on something. The successful businesses, on the other hand, kept trying things. They'd plan as best they could briefly, but once they had eighty percent of the idea together, they put it in motion, instead of laboring to figure out the remaining twenty percent and then have the idea fail anyway.

These businesses that were willing to try things quickly learned that "chaotic action is preferable to orderly inaction." A favorite axiom among them is "Do it, fix it, try it," or as one blue chip company spokesman put it, "Ready, fire, aim."

We did something like that ourselves recently. We noticed that we don't have much going on for the young adults in our church. Having a year-round Sunday school class didn't seem feasible because several of the people in that age group are off to college during the year. But it occurred to us that a lot are home for the summer. So why not a summer class? Within a space of just a few weeks of when we got the idea, we sent letters to the potential class members, we secured a teacher, and we set a start date. And we had a class all summer with young adults present every week.

Now maybe there was a better way to do it. But rather than debate it and debate it, we tried something, and it worked pretty well. In fact, well enough that we'll probably do it again next summer. We've got a few plans for some things between now and then too.

In most cases, trying something that might work is better than going on and on about how hard the problem is.

When we consider the scope of our own problems or the things we feel God is asking us to do, *try* becomes an important word. God doesn't ask us to try alone, but to try with his help. So often, making an attempt when we feel called by God is rewarding for not just ourselves but for others.

There's a wonderful story involving the great pianist, Paderewski. A mother, wishing to encourage her young son's progress on the piano, took him to a Paderewski concert. After they were seated, the mother spotted a friend in the audience and, leaving her son in his seat, she walked down the aisle to talk to her. The boy, fascinated by the concert hall, got up and began to roam around, eventually coming to a door marked "No Admittance." He wandered in anyway. When the houselights dimmed, the mother returned to her seat to find her son missing. Just then the curtains parted, and to her horror, she saw her son sitting at the keyboard of the impressive Steinway grand piano on stage. He was sitting there innocently plucking out, "Twinkle, Twinkle, Little Star."

At that moment, Paderewski made his entrance and saw what was happening. He went over to the piano and said to the boy, "Don't quit. Keep playing." He then reached his left hand out and added a bass part to the boy's melody. Next he reached around the boy with his right arm and added a running obbligato, and together the boy and the grand master gave the audience a wonderful creative experience. The audience was mesmerized.

Most of the time when God calls us to try, I think he means we should do what Robert Raikes did — get in there and start plucking out the melody the best we can, and then trust God to add the chords that turn our efforts into a concerto.

We're back in Gloucester now, and the year is 1811. Robert Raikes has just ordered a new waistcoat and is looking forward to wearing it. He plans to have dinner with his brother. But death strikes suddenly, and the useful life of this warmhearted, far-seeing good man comes to an end. His coffin leaves the house borne on the shoulders of friends — a common practice in that day.

What is not common, however, is that a large crowd of children precedes his coffin to the church where the funeral will take place. They were some of those introduced to the faith and given a better chance at life — all because Bobby Wildgoose tried.

Stan Purdum

Reformation Day

Service Of Worship

Reformation Sunday

Welcome and Announcements

Prelude

Call to Worship

Leader: This God — his way is perfect;
People: **the promise of the Lord proves true;**
he is a shield for all who take refuge in him.
Leader: For who is God, but the Lord?
People: **And who is a rock, except our God?**
Leader: The God who has girded me with strength and
has opened wide my path.
People: **Let us praise God!**

— adapted from 2 Samuel 22:31-33

*Hymn   "A Mighty Fortress Is Our God"

*Opening Prayer

O Lord, we come to this time and this place from a week that
has had its share of demands, challenges, and for some of us, even
some rewards. We admit to being frazzled, distracted, not fully
present.

Break through all that keeps us from hearing you, O God. Fill
our minds with your Word and our hearts with a desire to serve
you.

Accept our praise. In the name of Jesus. Amen.

*Praise Chorus   "Lord, Be Glorified"

Old Testament   Psalm 31:1-16

Presentation of Tithes and Offerings
  Offertory
  *Doxology

Morning Prayer
  O God of all times and places, we pray for your church, which is set today amid the perplexities of a changing order, and face to face with new tasks, and we pray that we who compose its ranks may serve you wholeheartedly.
  Baptize us afresh with the life-giving spirit of Jesus.
  Bestow upon us a great responsiveness to duty, a swifter compassion upon suffering, and an utter loyalty to your will.
  Help us to proclaim boldly the coming of your kingdom.
  Put upon our lips the vibrant Gospel of our Lord.
Fill us with the prophets' scorn of tyranny, and with a Christlike tenderness for the heavyladen and the downtrodden.
  Make us valiant to serve our fellow human beings, that, like Jesus the crucified Lord, we may mount by the path of the cross to a higher glory; through Jesus Christ our Lord. Amen.
                    — Walter Raushenbush (1861-1918), altered

Hymn   "Break Thou The Bread Of Life"

New Testament   Romans 5:1-10

Choir Anthem

Sermon   Facing The 21st Century With A 16th-Century Faith

*Hymn   "My Hope Is Built"

*Benediction

Postlude

16

Facing The 21st Century
With A 16th-Century Faith

Romans 5:1-10

Well, here we are in the last week of October. What does the world seem like to you these days? Last week, I happened to be talking with a couple of friends about the state of things. The conversation ranged over some of the things that had happened within the last year or so, beginning with 9/11 and including the anthrax letters, the possible war with Iraq, the new revelations about North Korea having an atomic weapons program, and now the sniper [the two men had not been caught yet]. One of my friends said, "I can't think of a time when things have been so messed up!"

The other man, who is a bit of a historian, said, "Oh, I don't know. The Thirty Years War (1618-1648) that ravaged central Europe and especially Germany in the seventeenth century must have seemed pretty horrible to people living then."

A day later I was reading a magazine and saw an article titled "The Eve of Destruction, Then and Now."[1] It was about how forty years ago — specifically the last week of October 1962 — at the time of the Cuban Missile Crisis, it appeared that America was on the brink of nuclear war with the Soviet Union. Some people were stockpiling groceries and building bomb shelters.

I mention both of these things for perspective, as a reminder that history is filled with dangerous times. And despite them, or perhaps because of them, Christianity has proved a durable faith that has helped people deal with the threats and dangers of life.

While of course Christianity itself was born in the first century A.D. during the time Jesus walked the earth, the form of Christianity we proclaim today has a lot to do with something that happened in the sixteenth century, during what's been called the Protestant Reformation.

17

That also was an event from the last week of October — specifically, October 31, 1517. Thus the last Sunday in October has sometimes been observed in Protestant churches as Reformation Sunday. That late October day, nearly 500 years ago, a sturdy and devout Catholic monk by the name of Martin Luther walked to the chapel of the University of Wittenberg in Germany and tacked a paper to the chapel door. This paper contained 95 statements — points for discussion — regarding the then current state of the church.

Luther had no idea that this action was to touch off a movement that would radically alter both the shape of history and the future of the church. In fact, it was a common practice to use the chapel door as a kind of bulletin board where issues for debate could be posted. What happened, however, was that Luther's "95 Theses" struck a raw nerve, for they challenged some corruption and superstition in the medieval church.

The church in that day held tremendous power over people's lives. The threat of excommunication struck fear into the hearts of the common people. For some, the priesthood had become a way to money and power, and sometimes the upper church offices were sold to the highest bidder.

The immediate issue that seems to have prompted Luther's action was the sale of "indulgences." An indulgence was supposed to be a decree canceling the punishment still due after a sin was forgiven, and the church was the dispenser of these indulgences. However, sometimes instead of just granting the indulgences, priests would make people pay for them. In fact, people could even buy indulgences for a sin they had not yet committed, or to get a dead person out of purgatory and into heaven.

A Dominican monk by the name of Tetzel was even more enterprising. He traveled around Germany hawking indulgences using a slogan worthy of Madison Avenue: "As soon as coin in coffer rings / a soul from purgatory springs." (The public did not know that half of this money went to pay a debt that Albert of Brandenburg had acquired in purchasing the top church office in Germany.)

But in addition to indulgences, there were theological issues that troubled Luther as well. Luther had entered the monastery initially because he was extremely conscious of his own sinfulness. He thought that if he could live very devoutly and piously and do enough good works, he might eventually earn God's forgiveness. In fact, that was what the church was teaching in Luther's day.

Luther spent long hours in prayer. He would go to confession more often than others and sometimes stay as long as six hours. He would confess even the most trivial things he could think of and if, after leaving confession, he remembered some tiny thing he had forgotten to mention, he would be tortured by its memory for hours. He fasted for three days at a time and would sleep in the freezing cold with no blankets, all to make himself worthy.

He was, in short, a model monk. He did everything and more that the medieval church said was necessary for absolution from his sins. Yet, he was still overwhelmed by a feeling of his own unworthiness. He felt that he was under God's wrath and all of his devout efforts only intensified his distress.

A turning point came for Luther when the church appointed him to teach theology at the University of Wittenberg. Generally the church did not encourage Bible reading, but Luther had to read it in connection with the teaching. He discovered that the scriptures were more interesting than he had supposed. One day, while reading Romans, he came across these words: "we are justified by faith...."

These things were part of the backdrop that led Luther to post his disagreements with the church on the Wittenberg chapel door. To Luther's surprise, the 95 theses created an immense sensation, and in time, the furor over his statements led to a direct confrontation between Luther and the Pope. In 1521, Luther was excommunicated and his teachings were labeled heretical. At one point he had to go into hiding because some sought his life.

Luther and the many who followed him protested against much that the medieval church stood for, and as a result, they came to be called "Protesters" or "Protestants."

Now it should be recognized that the Catholic Church has long since corrected the abuses against which Luther spoke. Today many Catholic scholars recognize Luther's contributions with respect.

Also, we need to see that we who are Protestants have much more in common with Catholics than we used to think. Today the Catholic Church leads millions into real fellowship with Christ and we recognize them as our brothers and sisters in the faith.

In the view of Protestantism, Luther's theology was not so much a brand new thing as it was a rediscovery of the teachings of the New Testament. But the timing in history of Luther's life and the energy he threw into his protest made his 95 theses the basis of a religious revolution.

It is instructive for us to look at Luther's major points of difference with the medieval church because those issues are the basis not only for much of what we believe today, but also for how durable and strengthening our faith has been in the face of the dangers of life.

Luther himself gave a great testimony to the sustaining power of faith in Christ in the words of his great hymn, the one we sang at the opening of our service today, "A Mighty Fortress Is Our God." Listen to these words from the hymn:

> And though this world with devils filled should threaten
>   to undo us,
> We will not fear, for God hath willed his truth to tri-
>   umph through us.
> The Prince of Darkness grim, we tremble not for him;
> His rage we can endure, for lo, his doom is sure;
> One little word shall fell him.

We could read that first line as "And though this world with terrorists filled," or "with madmen with bombs filled," but that would not negate the faith declared in the song.

Also, note that the song does not tell us what that one little word is, but of course, it is "Jesus."

While Luther's 95 statements deal with many specific points of disagreement, there are three overarching issues that Luther raised and which have become the foundation of Protestant Christianity.

The first of these is the authority of the Bible.

In Luther's day, the Bible was available only in Latin and as such, could only be read by scholars, priests, and other persons of learning. Indeed, even if the common people had been able to read Latin, the church discouraged them from reading the Bible. Instead, they were taught to rely upon the church to tell them what was important for them to know from the scriptures. Thus, the church and its leaders became the supreme authorities for Christian life.

Luther, however, had found the real answer to his search for peace with God through reading the Bible. He came to see that the church was not teaching the whole message of the Bible and in fact it was mistaken in some of what it was teaching. For Luther, the Bible became a higher authority than the church. In time, he insisted that every Christian was competent to interpret the scriptures himself or herself without the aid of clergy, but helped by the Holy Spirit.[2]

Such was Luther's belief in the importance of the Bible that he devoted a great deal of time to translating the Bible into the language of the common people. And his translation is still the primary one used in Germany today.

The Bible became the touchstone of reformation Christianity and made possible the rediscovery of the fundamentals of New Testament faith.

The second overarching issue Luther raised is what has been termed "the priesthood of all believers."

The priest in Luther's day was looked upon almost as a "superhuman." He was the one who spoke to God on behalf of others. He was an intercessor and people confessed to him — he spoke to God for them.

Some of the priests were corrupt and charged fees for their services. They instilled great fear in the common people by threatening not to intercede with God for them if they did not conform to the church's wishes. This is what made excommunication so terrible. The one excommunicated felt completely separated from God, for the church was seen as the only way to be saved.

But even when the priests were sincere believers, and not corrupt, Luther felt that too much authority was granted to them and as such, the priests could actually be an impediment in the search for salvation.

21

Luther taught that every Christian was his own priest and could have fellowship with God on his own without benefit of clergy. He said that through faith, each person could confess his or her sins to God and receive forgiveness from God without the intersession of the church. Every person could get right with God, be forgiven by faith, without conforming to the church's additional requirements.[3]

Thus in the Protestant churches, we generally have not priests but ministers. In Luther's view, the minister was a person who had been called to instruct and lead in the faith, but not be an intermediary between the individual and God.

Luther's third issue was the belief in justification by faith.

The medieval church taught that if one did certain prescribed "works," salvation could be earned. This had been the reason for Luther's careful attention to fasting, confession, and so forth.

On one occasion, while still in his searching period, Luther went to the Scala Santa, a church in Rome, and climbed the steps on his knees, saying the Lord's Prayer on every step. He did this to deliver his grandfather from purgatory. But when he got to the top step a question flashed across his mind, "Who knows whether this is true?"[4]

Luther, of course, after his awakening would have no more to do with such practices, for the Bible convinced him that we are reconciled with God through faith and faith alone.

Luther spoke of "justification by faith alone," with the word "alone" being his addition to Paul's phrase "justification by faith." Luther believed that the word "alone" conveyed the real intention of the Pauline expression and therefore felt that it helped one to understand the meaning more accurately.

Essentially, when Luther spoke of justification, he meant that God gave righteousness to humans who reach for it in faith, that righteousness was a gift of God, totally undeserved by humankind and beyond our reach; therefore it could only come from God, from outside of humanity's own resources. Thus when Luther spoke of justification by faith alone, he meant that there were no good works, acts of penitence, or any other deeds whereby we could earn or deserve righteousness. It had instead to be a free gift from a sovereign God, who himself chose to give it.

22

By "faith" Luther meant an act of acceptance of this gift, an act that he called the "great exchange." That is, I give Christ my sin and he gives me his righteousness.

We might illustrate Luther's thought by saying that righteousness is like a cloak that only God can give to cover a man and that in accepting this cloak, the man must be willing to give God the dirty rags, representing sins, that he has been wearing.

Luther stated this understanding of justification in a preface he wrote to the book of Romans.[5] Some 200 years later, a man, who was every bit as distressed about his spiritual condition as Luther had been, heard Luther's preface to Romans being read in a worship service. As Luther's words hit home, that man felt his heart strangely warmed by the assurance of God's salvation. His name was John Wesley; he went on to found Methodism, and through him, Luther's rediscovery of New Testament salvation was introduced to yet another group of people.

The Reformation reminds us of the power of our faith for living in dangerous times.

Luther affirmed the authority of the Bible. Thus we need read it and let its words soak into our souls and minds. Reading the Bible is not just a nice idea; it is a vital link to God through which he speaks to us.

Luther told us that we are each our own priest. Thus we need to pray. The church priests of Luther's day listened to a person's confessions and then they prayed to God on that person's behalf. Luther said that God was approachable and that we did not need an intermediary. We can each come to him and he will grant absolution. But to come to him, we need to pray.

Luther found the only basis for a life of peace with God to be justification by faith alone. Thus, while we believe in doing good, we must not rely upon good deeds to bring us forgiveness, but upon the grace of God through Jesus Christ. Good deeds are the fruit of a forgiven life and not the means of obtaining it.

Read the Bible, pray, trust God for our salvation. These lessons come to us out of history, but the experiences of Christians through the ages have shown them to be mighty things in facing a dangerous world. And that is just as true in this twenty-first century as it was in the sixteenth.

Stan Purdum

---

1. Bruce Handy and Glynis Sweeny, *Time*, October 28, 2002, p. 76.

2. On one occasion, a cardinal was trying to make Luther recant what he had said about the Bible. He reminded Luther that the pope was the interpreter of scripture. Luther replied, "His Holiness abuses scripture. I deny that he is above scripture." Later, given one last chance to recant, Luther said: "Unless I am convicted by scripture and plain reason — I do not accept the authority of popes and councils, for they have contradicted each other — my conscience is captive to the Word of God. I cannot and will not recant anything, for to go against conscience is neither right nor safe. God help me." (Roland H. Bainton, *Here I Stand: A Life of Martin Luther* [New York: Meridian, 1995], p. 144.)

3. Luther's own words on the matter are: "All of us who have been baptized are priests without distinction, but those whom we call priests are ministers chosen from among us that they should do all things in our name, their priesthood is nothing but a ministry." (Bainton, p. 106.)

4. Robert Hasting Nichols, *The Growth of the Christian Church* (Philadelphia: Westminster Press, 1941), p. 184.

5. In his preface to the epistle of Romans, Luther wrote: "Faith is a living and unshakable confidence, a belief in the grace of God that a man would die a thousand deaths for its sake. This kind of confidence in God's grace ... makes us joyful, high-spirited, and eager in our relations with God and with all mankind ... Hence, the man of faith, without being driven, willingly and gladly seeks to do good to everyone, serve everyone, suffer all kinds of hardships for the sake of the love and glory of the God who has shown him such grace." (*Martin Luther's Preface to the Epistle of St. Paul to the Romans* [Nashville: Discipleship Resources, 1977], p. 7.)

All Saints' Day

Service Of Worship

All Saints' Sunday

Welcome and Announcements

Prelude

Call to Worship
Leader: With people from all times and places,
People: God calls us to worship him.
Leader: In company with those well-known and little known,
People: God invites us into his presence.
Leader: Along with those of great faith and those struggling to believe,
People: God offers his Son as the way, the truth, and the life.
Leader: Let us praise God.
People: Let us praise God indeed!

*Hymn   "Forward Through The Ages"

*Opening Prayer
Loving God, as we come to worship:
    unblock our ears that we may hear you;
    unclog our minds that we may understand you;
    unglue our voices that we may praise you;
    unlock our hearts that we may serve you.
Amen.

*Praise Chorus   "Holy Ground"

*Affirmation of Faith   The Apostles' Creed

Hymn   "Awake My Soul, Stretch Every Nerve"

Presentation of Tithes and Offerings
   Offertory
   *Doxology

Morning Prayer
   O God, we give you thanks for all those through the ages who have trusted you, and who now abide in your heavenly presence. A few of them achieved fame, but most went unrecorded, except in your Book of Life. To be sure, they were human, but with the aid of your Spirit, they did great deeds of mercy and offered strong witness to your power and love.
   We thank you, too, O God, especially for those who loved and served you within the fellowship of this congregation. Especially now we remember those who transferred to the kingdom triumphant this past year, including [names of persons who died in last twelve months].
   And we thank you also that you still call people from every nation and every race and every tongue to come to your kingdom. Help us so to live that we, too, may be counted among your saints.
   In the name of Jesus. Amen.

New Testament   Hebrews 11:32—12:2

Choir Anthem

Sermon   Running With The Cloud

***Hymn**   "For All The Saints"

***Benediction**

Postlude

Running With The Cloud

Hebrews 11:32—12:2

What term do you use to identify yourself as a person who is a disciple of Jesus Christ? Most often, I use the word "Christian." Some people prefer to call themselves "born-again Christians" or "believers," but in reality, those are both synonyms for the simpler word, Christian. But I'd like to suggest one more term that you might not have considered: *saint*. The next time someone asks you about your faith, you can tell them you are a saint.

Now I can guess that not one of you is actually going to do that. I mean, just imagine what would happen if, in front of the guys at work, you announced that you are a saint. After all, it's hard enough for most of us at work to say that we are a Christian, let alone a saint.

But in addition to not using the term because of the probable ridicule we'd face, we're also reluctant to label ourselves as saints because we don't believe we are. In today's parlance, "saint" is usually reserved for someone like the late Mother Teresa or maybe Bishop Tutu or Billy Graham, but not for persons such as ourselves. The word seems to imply an almost superhuman quality of holiness, the ability to be so self giving that most of us simply wouldn't qualify. Also, we often think of a saint as someone who's dead.

But the New Testament actually uses the word to identify living followers of Jesus Christ. For example, when Paul wrote his first letter to the Christians at Corinth, he began as follows: "To the church of God that is in Corinth, to those who are sanctified in Christ Jesus, called to be saints, together with all those who in every place call on the name of our Lord Jesus Christ ..." (1 Corinthians 1:2). For another example, and there are many in the New Testament, read Acts 9.

Most of the time, when the New Testament used the word *saints*, it was referring to people who were very much alive right then. They were people who were far from perfect. In fact, in the case of the first letter to the Corinthians, Paul was writing because of some unholy things going on in the church. Nonetheless, Paul called those followers of Jesus saints, not for being perfect, but for being redeemed.

In the centuries since, we come to prefer our saints to have already passed on, as this little bit of anonymous rhyme suggests:

To live above with the saints we love, that is purest glory.
But to live below with the saints we know, ah, that's
another story.

On the church's calendar, November 1 is called All Saints' Day, with observance of it being on the Sunday nearest to that date. In the high liturgical churches, All Saints' is a major observance. In the lower liturgical churches, All Saints' is an optional service. Personally, while never a fan of high liturgy, I think we can benefit from thinking together about the meaning of the day.

The observance apparently had it roots in Rome, some 1,400 years ago, when a number of Christians gathered the physical remains of a number of unknown Christians who had died martyrs' deaths and dedicated an old Roman temple, the Pantheon, in their memory. Pope Boniface IV, who presided over the dedication, declared the day All Saints' and directed that it be celebrated annually to honor not only Christian martyrs, but also all who in any time or country lived and died for Christ. It became, in fact, a kind of Christian Memorial Day.

But here's the wrinkle, and it gets at why you should care about what this day represents. The major feature of All Saints' Day is that it honors our Christian predecessors not just as the dead in Christ, but in the strong confidence that they are *alive with Christ* forever. And as such, they are there cheering us on as we run the race of life.

In one sense, we can easily understand that, for we recognize that in this life, we benefit every day from inventions and advances in medicine from people who lived in earlier generations. For example, on any list of great scientists of the past, the name of Sir Isaac Newton is bound to appear. Among other things, he formulated the law of gravity and invented differential calculus. He had a brilliant mind, but with true humility he once observed, "If I have seen farther, it is because I stood on the shoulders of giants." He was acknowledging the debt he owed to those who had blazed the trail in science and mathematics before him.

But in our reading for today, the author of Hebrews gives us a different idea. The whole of chapter 11 is a kind of roll call of heroes of the faith: Abel, Enoch, Noah, Abraham, Sarah, Isaac, Jacob, Rahab, Gideon, Barak, Samson, David, Samuel, and others. When the author of Hebrews finishes this list, he begins chapter 12 with these words: "Therefore, since we are surrounded by so great a cloud of witnesses, let us also lay aside every weight and the sin that clings so closely, and let us run with perseverance the race that is set before us...."

The Hebrews writer apparently pictured the living saints — Christians — of his day as running the race of life, but not running it alone. Instead, they were running in the presence of saints from the past, this "cloud of witnesses," who, having finished their own races, have gone to sit in the viewing stands to cheer on those who are still running.

That is the great idea of All Saints' Day — one life following after and strengthening itself by other lives that have gone before it. In my family, for example, I am the fourth generation to be in the ministry. It means something to me to know that my parents, who thankfully are still living, pray for me and encourage me in my work. But it also means something to know that my grandfather, who died when I was twelve, and my grandmother, who was also a minister and died just a few years ago, are now rooting for me from the heavenly bleachers. It even means something to me that my great-grandparents, who died before I was born, are in those bleachers too, cheering my success.

A few years ago, I read an account by Exie Wilde Henson in the little devotional book, *The Upper Room*, where she wrote about being asked to lead a prayer seminar. She didn't think of herself as a skillful leader, but before saying no, she decided to seek guidance in prayer. She prayed, "Lord, if my mother were alive to pray for me, I would feel confident enough to do this." Henson wrote that God assured her that her mother's prayers were still being answered.[1] Her mother is no doubt one of those in the stands cheering for Ms. Henson as she runs the race of life.

But it's not just our direct ancestors the author of Hebrews had in mind; it's the whole body of believers who lived and died in a state of faithfulness to God who are now watching us and calling out heavenly encouragement. We who hold the Christian faith today do so because it was handed down to us by faithful witnesses who lived before us.

Sometimes that linkage with the church of the past is fairly direct. In 1858, a Sunday school teacher by the name of Kimball led a Boston shoe clerk to Christ. That clerk, whose name was Dwight L. Moody, became an evangelist. In 1879, while holding a crusade in England, Moody awakened the evangelistic zeal of Frederick B. Meyer, the pastor of a small church. Later, Meyer, preaching on an American campus, brought a student named J. Wilber Chapman to Christ. Chapman, in turn, while working for the YMCA, employed Billy Sunday to do evangelistic work. Sunday so inspired a group of North Carolina men that after Sunday's campaign, they brought another evangelist to town. The person they brought was Mordecai Hamm, who in his preaching there led to Christ a young man by the name of Billy Graham.

You see, what all of this means is that the church universal never consists of only the Christians who happen to be alive on earth at any one time. That is what theologians call the church "militant." This comes from the idea that the church in the world is the body that is at war with the powers of evil that obstruct the purposes of God. Living Christians cannot rest as long as there is injustice, bigotry, hate, conflict, abuse, and so forth in the society. We here are all part of the church militant.

But there is also what theologians call the Church "triumphant," that part of the church made up of all the believers from the beginning of the world who now rest from their labors. That part of the church which is not fighting evil any longer, but which is now fully participating in the triumph that Christ has won for the whole church on the cross. The church on earth exists supported and surrounded by the church triumphant, but the church itself includes both realities.[2]

There's an old hymn that expresses this idea. It says:

> *The church triumphant in thy love,*
> *Their mighty joys we know;*
> *They sing the Lamb in hymns above,*
> *And we in hymns below.*[3]

I want to be clear that the church does not support any of that foolishness called spiritualism, including any of that nonsense about people communicating with the dead through so-called mediums or séances or any other methods. Rather, we are simply pointing out the church of Christ has no end. Death cannot destroy it.

During WWI, a regiment of English soldiers was billeted in a French village. The English colonel, a cynical man, enjoyed poking fun at the village priest. One Sunday morning, the colonel passed the church as a handful of people were leaving after the service. He said to the priest, "Good morning, Father. Not many at Mass this morning. Not very many." The priest answered, "No, my son, you are wrong. Thousands and thousands and tens of thousands." And he was right.

Earlier in the service, we affirmed our faith using the historic words of the Apostles' Creed. Among the things we said was, "I believe in the communion of saints." This phrase can have two meanings. It can refer to the communion Christians share in the Lord's Supper. But it also refers to the unity between the church militant and the church triumphant.

A young boy was asked by his Sunday school teacher what he thought a saint was. As he thought about the question, he happened to remember a large church he had visited with his parents the previous summer. There he had seen some of the saints of old depicted in the stained-glass windows. Finally he replied, "A saint is someone who lets the light shine through." That's at least one aspect of what the race of life is for Christians, to let the light of God shine through us.

And what is that light? If we go back to the book of Hebrews, we find the answer. In chapter 11, we read about some people that the author of Hebrews identifies as "saints." If you know your Old Testament history, you may have been surprised at some of the people who made this particular list. There was Jacob, who for a good part of his life was a sneaky swindler; Noah, who was a known drunk; Rahab the prostitute; David the adulterer; Samson the self-centered, and so on. Actually, none of those on the list were noted for moral perfection. But we only read the final verses of chapter 11. If you go back and read the first two verses of that chapter, here's what it says: "Now faith is the assurance of things hoped for, the conviction of things not seen. Indeed, by faith our ancestors received approval." In other words, what makes them saints is not the record of their achievements, but that when it came down to a crucial moment, they each chose to follow a course that was in line with the purposes of God. They had faith. The light that shines through them is the light of faith.

And that's why we, too, can legitimately be called saints. If we have faith in God, if we really trust and obey him in the crucial moments of life, we too are saints.

As I said earlier, you may not want to call yourself a saint in front of your fellow workers, but if they are watching, they may be able to see the light of faith through you.

So as we run the race of life, let us take heart that we do so in the presence of the cloud of witnesses, those people of God who lived before us and who now have finished their own races. They have not retreated to the heavenly locker rooms, but are back in the bleachers for our benefit. We knew we had their example and their wisdom — as passed down in writings from the past — but now we know we also have their encouragement and can live by faith, as they did. We run, not with the crowd that ignores the way of God, but with the cloud that ran with him.

Stan Purdum

---

1. *The Upper Room*, July-December 1983, p. 68.

2. See George W. Forell, *The Protestant Faith,* pp. 200-201.

3. Charles Wesley, "Happy The Souls To Jesus Joined," *The Book of Hymns*, p. 535.

Thanksgiving

Service Of Worship

Thanksgiving

Welcome and Announcements

Prelude

Call to Worship
Leader: The Lord is clothed with honor and majesty,
People: Wrapped in light as with a garment.
Leader: He makes the clouds his chariot,
People: And rides on the wings of the wind.
Leader: God set the earth on its foundations,
People: So that it shall never be shaken.
Leader: Let us worship God.
People: Let us worship him indeed!

                      — adapted from Psalm 104

*Hymn   "We Gather Together"

*Opening Prayer
    Almighty God, we gather together to worship you, believing that somehow the assembling of ourselves in joint worship pleases you and helps us grow in our faith individually. Together we praise your name and ask you to make your will known to us. Help us in this service to set aside the things that distract us from listening for your word. Enable the things we say and do in these moments to become channels for your word of truth to come to us. Through Jesus we pray. Amen.

Choruses
    "Fill My Cup, Lord"
    "He Is Lord"

Giving Thanks
[Here invite anyone who wishes to stand and express thanks for some blessing that has come to them]

Prayer of Thanksgiving
God of all blessings, we thank you for the riches of your love that you have showered upon us this year past. And thank you for the richness of your presence that was with us even when we passed through dark valleys and deep troughs. Accept now our thanksgiving and our praise, from our lips and from our hearts. In the name of Jesus. Amen.

Chorus   "Alleluia"

Presentation of Tithes and Offerings
    Offertory
    *Doxology

Men's Chorus   "Now Thank We All Our God"
[Just use the regular arrangement from your hymnbook; this hymn is very effective when sung by male voices]

Scripture   Isaiah 41:8-10; 43:1-7

Sermon   A Solid Place To Stand

*Hymn   "How Firm A Foundation"
[Verses are sung, interspersed in sermon, but sing first verse again now]

*Benediction

Postlude

A Solid Place To Stand

Isaiah 41:8-10; 43:1-7

Of all the holidays of the year, Thanksgiving is my favorite. One thing I like is that is comes quietly, without a lot of hoopla. There is none of the hurry and scurry of preparation as there is at Christmas. There is no decking out in new clothes as we sometimes do for Easter. Generally speaking, unless you're a turkey farmer, you probably do not arrive at Thanksgiving all exhausted from weeks of preparation.

I also like it that the day is a time for families to gather and spend time together.

The history of Thanksgiving also interests me. I am impressed by the fact that the first Thanksgiving was held by people (the ones we call Pilgrims) who had first gone through a terrible winter and suffered appalling losses. Despite this, by the time they got to the end of their first growing season, they gathered to thank God for being with them throughout it all.

The fact is, the Pilgrims arrived in the new world at the wrong time of year and in the wrong place. They were heading for the area we now call Virginia, but instead landed at what is now Provincetown, Massachusetts, on November 21, 1620. It was the beginning of winter and they faced that harsh season without adequate supplies. Half their number died that first winter, including thirteen out of the eighteen wives who came on the Mayflower. Many more would have died except that they found some caches of food stored by the Indians, and helped themselves.

At one point, only six of the settlers were well enough to nurse the others. And when people died, their comrades buried them in unmarked graves so that the Indians would not know how few of them were left.

Things got a little better the following year. Crops were planted, homes were improved, and when the harvest was in, there was a time of giving thanks to God for what they had, and more remarkably, *for being with them through the ordeal.*

Actually, the promise of God's presence is a consistent theme in the Bible, and certainly one that scripture for today emphasizes.

> *Do not fear, for I am with you, do not be afraid, for I am your God; I will strengthen you, I will help you, I will uphold you with my victorious right hand.*
>
> — Isaiah 41:10

> *When you pass through the waters, I will be with you; and through the rivers, they shall not overwhelm you; when you walk through fire you shall not be burned, and the flame shall not consume you.*   — Isaiah 43:2

Along with some verses from Hebrews and 2 Timothy, these words from Isaiah were part of the inspiration for one of our best hymns, "How Firm A Foundation." The hymn first appeared in 1787 in a hymnbook published in London by John Rippon, a Baptist pastor, but we don't know for sure who the author was. He is identified only as "K," and some historians think it may have been a man named Thomas Keen, who was the music director in Rippon's church.

Let's sing verse 1. [All sing]

Note that this first verse says that this firm foundation has been laid down for us "in his excellent word," that is, the Bible. Let's look at how that is true.

- In Genesis, when God first called Abraham, he promised to be with him.
- That promise was repeated to Abraham's son Isaac (Genesis 26:3): "Reside in this land as an alien, and I will be with you, and will bless you."
- It was repeated again to Isaac's son Jacob (Genesis 28:15): "Know that I am with you and will keep you wherever you go."

- Later still to Moses, who, when he was called to lead the people of Israel out of Egypt, protested that he was inadequate. God said to him: "I will be with you" (Exodus 3:12).
- Moses must have found that to be true, because later, when Moses was near the end of his life and was handing over the leadership of the people to Joshua, Moses told Joshua: "It is the Lord who goes before you. He will be with you; he will not fail you or forsake you. Do not fear or be dismayed" (Deuteronomy 31:8).
- Psalm 23 says: "Yea though I walk through the valley of the shadow of death, I will fear no evil, for thou art with me."
- Years later, King David repeated the promise to his son, Solomon: "Be strong and of good courage, and act. Do not be afraid or dismayed; for the Lord God, my God, is with you. He will not fail you or forsake you" (1 Chronicles 28:20).
- I could easily go on and give you examples where the promise of God's presence was repeated to the Psalmist, to Isaiah, to Jeremiah, to Paul, and to many others.
- Jesus himself, as he approached his death, said, "I am not alone, for the Father is with me" (John 16:32).
- And then, in the very last book of the Bible, the promise shows up again. In the vision of John of Patmos, he foresees a "new Jerusalem," and hears a loud voice that says, "See, the home of God is among mortals. He will dwell with them as their God; they will be his peoples, and God himself will be with them" (Revelation 21:3).

So, you see, the hymnwriter wasn't just being poetic. He was stating the reality that the Bible — "his excellent word" — lays a firm foundation for our faith that God is present with us.

You've occasionally heard claims that faithfulness to God will bring health, wealth, and happiness, but, frankly, that is not the promise of the Bible. What the Bible does promise is God himself. His presence will be with us. To which the hymn writer adds, "What more can he say?" That was the truth that the Pilgrims celebrated on the first Thanksgiving.

Let's sing verse 2. [All sing]

Let us not discount the importance of God's presence. I was reminded of that the other day when I read about a certain father who went to visit his son's preschool. It was a day when dads could come to visit. But when he got there, he was surprised to discover that only a handful of fathers had come to be with their children. Later in that morning, all the children were sitting on the floor in a circle. The teacher asked the children to tell the group something about their fathers, something that was special. One little boy said, "Well, my daddy is a lawyer. He makes a lot of money and we live in a big house." Another child said, "My father is very smart. He teaches at the college and a lot of important people know him." When it was time for this father's son to say something special about his dad, the little boy looked up at his father, then he looked around the circle of his friends, and then he just smiled and proudly said, "My dad ... my dad is here!"

Or, in the words of Cynthia Heimel, "Do not look for [God] in the heavens; he only keeps a small locker there, only goes there to change" (*But Enough About You* [New York: Simon & Schuster, 1986], p. 70).

Okay, you agree. God was with the faithful people of the Bible and with the Pilgrims, and because we accept the faith in Christ, the promise of God's presence is made to us as well.

But so what? What does it really mean on a nitty-gritty, every-day level that God is with us?

For one thing, it means that we cannot sin in peace. We can sometimes do things wrong and get away with them as far as other people are concerned. But the reality of God's presence means that our attitudes and deeds are open knowledge to God. In those cir-cumstances, there may be times when we'd just as soon not have God present. But think about the times when we've benefited from someone else's knowledge of God's presence. Perhaps they've been angry with us, and inclined to do something hateful against us, but their knowledge that God was present would not let them sin against us in peace, and a reconciliation was achieved.

But God's presence also means something else. And that is the subject of verses 3 and 4 of the hymn. Let's sing them. [All sing]

In the scriptures, deep water and fire are often metaphors for serious trouble and extreme danger. Sometimes they were also literal danger for the people of Israel. When they had to cross the Red Sea with the Egyptians in hot pursuit, they faced literal deep waters. When the three Hebrew young men refused to worship the Babylonian god, they were thrown into a literal furnace of fire. In both of these cases, God was with them. When they trusted that God was with them, they handled the danger.

What are the deep waters you face? There is a phenomenon that sometimes occurs during times of deep troubles where the most comfort comes from people who do little more than be present. Again and again, I've had people who have lost loved ones say that the people who seemed to add to their grief were those who tried to explain it, defend God, or tell them what they should do. The ones who were comforting were those who just showed up and grieved with them. God shows up.

There is yet another thing God's presence means, and verse 5 mentions it. Let's sing it. [All sing]

"That soul though all hell should endeavor to shake...." Some may take that to mean the working of a satanic power, but I think of more literal hells. Moments of true terror.

I talked once to a young woman who survived a terrible car crash. She was alone in her car when a large truck coming the other way went out of control and careened toward her. I asked her what she did. She said that in the split second when it was clear that she was going to be hit, she threw herself down on the front seat. And she added, "I think I screamed, 'Oh, my God.' "

"Oh, my God." What is that? A throwaway phrase? Mild profanity? I don't think so. In its barest form, it's a prayer. And what is there within us that causes such words to leap to our lips in moments of pure terror? For many, it is the conviction deep down that God really is present and is the only one who can confront the terror with us.

Do you know who John Dye is? He's the actor who plays Andrew, the angel of death, on the television series *Touched By An Angel*. (In a television interview recently he mentioned that he's noticed that when he flies on commercial airliners, some of the other passengers tend to get a little nervous.)

I've not seen that show often, but the few times I have, I've noticed that when Andrew comes to take someone out of this life, there is a recognition that this brings sadness to the person's family and friends, but not tragedy for the person. Andrew and his angel cohorts seem to understand that the death brings no interruption in the presence of God with the person.

Now I don't want to suggest that *Touched By An Angel* is a substitute for solid biblical theology, but I think the show has that point right, at least for those who trust God. The presence of God does not mean everything comes out as we want it to, or that God is some kind of guardian angel who snatches out of our path anything that might harm us. But it does mean that even losing our life does not deprive us of God's presence, which in its fullness, the Bible says, more than compensates for any troubles and loss in this life.

That's why the Pilgrims could celebrate and thank God despite the awful year they'd been through. And that's why we can too. The presence of God is a firm foundation — a solid place to stand.

Stan Purdum

Four Advent Monologues

Preface

Advent has never been my favorite preaching season. The lectionary begins by bringing us stories of tumult in the heavens. Then we get John the Baptist crunching down locusts while he stomps around in the wilderness preaching repentance. Or maybe we get some elevated metaphor, "the Word made flesh"; beautiful, but mysterious. Meanwhile, out in the pews, faces are looking puzzled. What about the manger? Aren't we going to hear about Mary and Joseph? Where are the Wise Men? And, most crucial of all, why are we singing all these funny hymns in a minor key instead of Christmas carols?

Finally, I threw lectionary purity to the wind. If I couldn't overcome the Christmas culture, I might as well use it to advantage.

Three of these monologues are an attempt to look at some of the key themes of Advent — watching, preparation, and righteous action — through the eyes of one of the characters in the Christmas drama. All are just ordinary people, finding their way through life, and trying to understand what the extraordinary happenings of that night might mean for them. The shepherd ponders why only he and his friends noticed the lights and music in the sky. Cousin Jochaved wonders how the Messiah came to be born in her home. (I worked with the understanding that "inn" is best translated "guest room.") And Joseph takes new risks and finds his life changed and expanded.

The last monologue grew out of a fascination with angels while I was in seminary. What would it be like to frighten people whenever you show up? Wouldn't it get rather tiresome? This Christmas angel is intrepid, funny, and *tired*!

Have fun with these. Although "Tidings" demands to be memorized, the others can be done with a manuscript in hand, if you wish.

Pamela J. Abbey

41

Joseph

The Measure Of A Man

Matthew 1:18-25

Measure twice; cut once.

That's been my life's motto, since my teens, I guess. I'm a carpenter like my father. He trained me, taught me, encouraged me. Sometimes he scolded me when I wasn't careful enough.

Carpentry is a precise trade. Just a tiny error while measuring can throw the whole project off. If you cut a piece of lumber too long, that's not so bad. You can always slice off a bit more. But if it's too short, then you have to set it aside, hoping it will be useful another time. That can get expensive.

Israel is not blessed with trees, you see. Much of our wood is imported from Lebanon. It's a necessity, but it's costly. And if I make a mistake, I have to absorb the cost. So I measure twice, cut once. I've become a careful man.

But I like my work. I love the feel and the smell of the wood. I like the process of creating something useful, something that will last. When I make a table for someone, I think about how it may be handed down from generation to generation. Just like my father handed down the trade of carpentry to me. My days are full of the smell of sawdust and the sounds of hammers and saws. When sunset comes, I look at my day's work — a table, a bench, a cart for a donkey to pull. It's plain, sturdy, and useful. It feels good.

I like my life. But, occasionally, I go to Jerusalem, to the Temple. I look at the beautiful wood there. The door frames are ornately carved. So are the beams in the ceiling. And they're inlaid with gold. Everything I do is useful and honest. But the things I make can't really be called beautiful. One table looks pretty much like the other.

When I go to Jerusalem and look at the Temple, I wonder what it would be like to build something just for the glory of God ... to

43

build something that didn't have a practical use. I wonder what that feels like.

There's not much chance of doing that in Nazareth. There's no Temple there and the people aren't rich. They can afford things that are well made, sturdy, and practical. Things that give good value. But there's not much call for things that are carved or decorative, things that exist simply to cheer the spirit.

I guess I'm as careful with my life as I am with my lumber. At least I have been until recently. Lately things have been ... well ... strange.

A little over a year ago I entered into a betrothal. My wife to be was a girl named Miriam. I didn't know her well. I'd seen her sitting with the women at the back of the synagogue. I have to say, she was good to look at. She came from a good family, too. So when my father said it was time to start my own family and suggested Miriam as a wife, I agreed quickly. My father had taught me a good and useful trade. I thought I could trust his judgment in family matters, too.

It *was* time to think about having my own family. Father was active in our carpentry business, but I could see him slowing down. I could see that in not too many years, I would need an apprentice, just as I had been an apprentice to him.

So the betrothal took place. It was a serious business and there was no backing out. No changing your mind. Although Miriam and I would not live together for a while, neither of us could break off the betrothal. Only death or divorce could end it. So I listened very carefully as all the documents were read to me. There were dowries and agreements from both families and I wanted to be sure that everything was in good order. Joining two people was an even more intricate process than joining two pieces of wood! Measure twice; cut once.

Everything seemed to be in order and I liked Miriam. A lot. She was shy with me at first. But even then I could see an underlying twinkle and a certain strength. I thought we'd be a good match. I began to spend more time with her, usually with her family around. When the time came to live together, I didn't want either of us to feel like we were living with a stranger. It was the right thing to do.

As time passed, it became more than the right thing to do. I really enjoyed being with her. She had spirit. I could see that she was a good and responsible daughter, but she also had a carefree quality that attracted me. I laughed more when I was with her. I relaxed when she was around. Father was always good at selecting the right wood. I guess he was just as good at selecting the right wife.

So when Miriam put her head into my carpentry shop one day, eyes twinkling, I was glad. My heart warmed up right away.

"Joseph, I have to talk to you. I've got some wonderful news."

I wondered what it could be. Nothing very exciting ever happened in Nazareth. The plans for our marriage ceremony were in place. What could have made her eyes dance like this?

"Joseph, you'll never guess! The most wonderful thing. I'm going to have a child!"

"Certainly we will some day, Miriam," I said. "That goes along with marriage."

"No, Joseph. Not some day. Right now!"

It didn't make any sense. I'd never done more than hold her hand.

"Miriam, are you sure you know what you're talking about? We aren't living together yet. You can't be having a baby."

"I know, I know. But this is God's child, Joseph. I had a vision, or something. I was told I was going to have a baby by the power of the Spirit. He'll be the Savior of our people. Isn't that wonderful?"

No, it was *not*. It was not wonderful.

I wasn't sure what it was, but wonderful it wasn't.

I continued to talk with her, and she continued to make no sense at all. She swore she hadn't been with another man. And she wouldn't give up this vision story. It was obvious that *she* believed what she was saying.

It seemed to me that I was either betrothed to a boldfaced liar, who was very good at it, or she was simply crazy. Neither was acceptable as a wife.

Finally, angry and confused, with a heart that felt like a stone, I sent her out of my shop. I didn't know what to do. I didn't know what God would want me to do. I listened carefully when the

Torah was read and the rabbis taught from it. Because I thought that my life, and making it a life pleasing to God, was even more important than my craft of fitting wood together, I'd always wanted my life to be as honest and sturdy and true as the things I made. So I paid attention to the rabbis. The Law was God's way of measuring lives. And I knew how important measuring was. Measure twice; cut once.

According to the Law of Moses, Miriam had committed adultery. Adultery could be punished by stoning to death. In truth, that didn't happen often. The rabbis leaned toward compassion. I was glad of that, because as miserable as I was, I didn't want Miriam dead.

But that only left divorce. Maybe with the help of her family we could send her to relatives in another town where her shame wouldn't seem so great.

I ached. My whole body seemed to hurt, not just my heart. My body seemed to be weeping even though my eyes were dry.

Miriam had delighted me. How could my judgment, and my father's, have been so poor? How could we have completely failed to take the measure of Miriam's character?

Then it occurred to me — there was a third option. I could go ahead and marry her. I could raise the child as my own. But even if we were married soon, the old ladies would count on their fingers. And I'd be living with a woman who was either a liar or crazy. I couldn't be married to a woman I didn't trust. And I'd always wonder who the child's father was.

No, I would have to divorce her. That was the only proper thing to do. I'd speak to her parents tomorrow. They'd be heartbroken. Together we'd find a way to end this as gracefully as possible, for everyone's sake.

It took a long time for sleep to come that night. But it finally did and I began to dream. At first the dreams were of Miriam and times we had enjoyed together. But then I began to dream of that wonderful wood in the Jerusalem Temple. That wood that was carved, and detailed, and rich. In my dream, the wood seemed even more real than when I had seen it for myself. It was richer and deeper. It almost seemed alive.

In spite of the grief that I'd taken to bed with me, as I saw that carved wood of the Temple in my dream, my heart lifted. I began to feel a strange kind of joy, unlike anything I'd ever felt before. I wanted to laugh and cry all at the same time.

And then I saw a face. It was strong and beautiful. I couldn't tell if it was a man or a woman. I was frightened, but I found I couldn't look away from it. Then the voice spoke, and it sounded as though it came from the forests of Lebanon.

"Joseph, son of Jacob. Go ahead, take Miriam as your wife. Raise this baby as your own. He is God's child. And you must name him Yeshua, for he will be the Savior of his people."

That strange joy welled up in me. I was laughing and crying. It was true. Miriam was not crazy! She was not a liar!

The face faded away, and again I saw the carvings. I slept on. And when I woke with the sun, my heart was still singing.

But the waking world made me wonder ... was the dream real? It had been a real dream! But was it true? Was God creating something new? Something as beautiful, intricate, and lovingly designed as those carvings in the Temple?

I'd never put much stock in dreams, although I knew others did. Dreams just didn't fit my "measure twice, cut once" way of life. But then it hit me — something so obvious, yet it had never really dawned on me before.

My father had named me Joseph, after our ancestor who was sold into slavery in Egypt. There, Joseph had lived by his dreams. Every time his back had been against the wall, a dream had saved him. I'd been named for a man to whom God had spoken in his dreams. My father had passed on to me the honest, plain craft of carpentry. Maybe he was trying to pass on something else as well.

The choice was getting clearer. I could measure twice and cut once and have a plain, sturdy, honest life.

Or I could take a chance. I could do it differently. And maybe I would have a life as beautiful and breathtaking as the carvings in Jerusalem.

I chose.

I went to see Miriam. This time I recognized the sparkle in her eyes. For I had it, too. It was the sparkle of those to whom God has given the vision of something new.

So we were married. Miriam has grown heavy. Some days the sparkle is dimmed. Tomorrow we set out for Bethlehem to be counted in the Roman census. I hope we manage to make it there and back before the baby comes.

Am I sure about what I've done? Am I certain of the dream?

No. I'm not certain or sure. Maybe as the child grows and I see what he becomes, maybe I'll be certain then. But maybe not.

I've decided that when it comes to the voice of God, measure twice and cut once doesn't work. Maybe the best we can do is to do the things that make us feel like those carvings in the Temple made me feel.

I built a cradle for the baby. I measured twice and cut once for each piece. It went together beautifully. It's sturdy and honest. It will take care of this baby and all the rest that Miriam and I will have together. It's as good a cradle as I ever made.

But I did something else this time. When I'd measured and cut and joined, I took out my knife and began to carve. This cradle will be more than sturdy and practical and honest. It will be beautiful. No reason, really. Just in praise of God and this baby.

Pamela J. Abbey

Cousin Jochaved

A Heart Prepared

Luke 2:6-7

I'm so glad that census is over. I knew when they announced it that things would be — well — interesting!

My family lives in Bethlehem. Always has. My grandparents, my great-grandparents, and my great-great-grandparents lived here. You get the picture. This town has been our home for generations.

Both of my parents came from large families with lots of brothers and sisters. So I have lots of aunts and uncles. It seems like I have thousands of cousins. There wasn't enough work in Bethlehem to sustain everybody in my family, and some had a sense of adventure. Many of my relatives moved away. I have cousins and second cousins and shirttail relatives all over Israel.

So when the Romans announced a census and said that everyone had to return to his family's hometown to register, I knew what would happen. People I hadn't seen in years, plus some I hadn't even met, would start showing up. And they would all need a place to stay.

I felt lucky. My husband Reuben did well. We have a nice house. There's a little guest room that we use for extra people — and sometimes death or birth. I liked that little room. I'd given birth to all five of my children there. It seemed like a warm, inviting, lively place to me.

Although I was worried about how I'd care for all these relatives arriving, I was looking forward to seeing them — especially the younger ones I'd never met but only heard about.

My sister, Abigail, also lives in Bethlehem and she went into high gear. I've always envied her. She has things so well together and orderly and beautiful. Her house is always neater than mine. She never burns her bread when she bakes. I burn mine every other day. Her two children are always clean and neat.

Sometimes when I go to synagogue I hear the rabbi read from the book of Proverbs. There's a description there of the good wife. It says, "She seeks wool and flax, and works with willing hands. She rises while it is still night and provides food for her household and tasks for her servant girls. Her lamp does not go out at night."

That was Abigail ... except for the servant girls, of course. Our family isn't that wealthy.

I wished I could be more like her, with everything so tidy and looking nice. Reuben just laughed at me. He said our life was just fine. He was happy. The children were happy. And then he always suggested that if Abigail had five children instead of two, maybe her life wouldn't be so orderly either.

When they announced the census, we both went right to work, each in our own way. I cleaned out our little guest room and Abigail cleaned out hers. But she even made new curtains for the window. She started to dry more fruits and she ground extra flour. She wanted to be prepared for whoever came.

So did I. Really! But every time I decided to grind extra flour or dry more fruit, something would happen. Like the morning our youngest, Eli, came running in with a baby bird that had fallen out of its nest. I was all set for the grinding. I'd set aside extra time and had extra grain. But instead, there I was trying to improvise a warm nest and figure out a way to feed this little creature.

And we did. It even lived, much to Reuben's amazement. Who knows where it's flying around these days.

But I never did grind the extra flour.

As the census grew near I was apprehensive. Abigail was prepared. Her house was ready. Me ... I just hoped for the best. Mainly I hoped that not too many people would show up at one time. If we could have known who was arriving when, it wouldn't have been so bad. But that was hard to know. People could try to send a message about their plans with another traveler. But messages were often forgotten or lost. And even when we knew someone was on the way, a sick animal, weather, or rumors of robbers on the road ahead could slow a traveler down. We never knew for sure when we'd have guests.

So the census started, slowly at first, with people arriving every three or four days. Abigail and I took turns putting up our relatives at first. But then things speeded up. Most nights we both had people in our guest room. I worried about having enough food to share. And I was always a little ashamed that my house wasn't as neat and nice as Abigail's. But it was so much fun seeing people I hadn't seen since I was a child! Our children had a great time. They loved meeting their cousins who'd come from far away. Great-aunts and uncles would sometimes have a sweet hidden under their robes, too. In fact, the children had so much fun, they became a little unruly. It was hard to get them to do their chores.

It was especially hard to get them to clean the front room each morning after the animals left. I'm sure it seems strange to you to hear me say that there were animals in the front room. But our homes were built with that in mind. The front room is level with the ground. The rest of the house is raised a bit. You see, it wasn't safe to leave a valuable donkey or ox outside all night. It might be stolen. So as we withdrew into the upper levels of the house to sleep, the animals would come into the front room of the house. They were safe there and they helped to keep the house warm with their bodies. It worked well.

But, of course, there was a bit of clean up to be done in the morning, so that the room would be usable by us during the day.

But excited children was really my only problem those days. The food always seemed to stretch enough to go around. No one but me seemed to mind that the house wasn't perfect.

So I was shocked one day when Abigail came to me nearly in tears. She said, "I can't take this anymore, Jochaved. There are just too many people coming. I can't keep up with it."

I didn't understand her. She was the one who was so well prepared. She had laid in extra food and fixed up her extra room so nicely. In truth, her house was even a little bigger than ours. It seemed to me that she was caring for her guests just fine. And then she said something that really shocked me, "Jochaved, maybe we could ask them to stay in the inn outside of town."

The inn! No one we knew stayed at inns. Decent folk would rather sleep outside. Inns were dirty and mostly thieves stayed there.

51

I couldn't believe she was saying such a thing and I told her so. The only kind of inn that family or friends should stay in were the little rooms in our homes.

So with assurances from me that she was doing just fine, and offers to help if she needed it, she dried her eyes. But I really didn't understand. She had been more ready than I was for all of this.

So the days and weeks of the census went on. I enjoyed myself. Abigail? I guess the best thing to say is that she coped. Clearly, she wasn't happy and her guests sensed it.

But things began to wind down. There was more time between guests again. I was glad, especially for Abigail's sake. And the children began to behave better, too!

But then came *that* day. Great-uncle Eliazer and Great-aunt Rebekah arrived. So did Aunt Sarah and Uncle Malachi. Now Great-uncle Eliazer and Great-aunt Rebekah were getting up in years. How they managed the trip, I'll never know. Frankly, it made me mad and if there had been a Roman official in sight, I would have given him a piece of my mind.

All four arrived at the same time and we had to decide where they would stay. I saw that tense look around Abigail's mouth and I knew she wasn't up for dealing with Eliazer and Rebekah. It looked like they might be requiring a little extra care, special foods and extra blankets and things. I wasn't sure how I'd manage, but I knew I would. I hoped they'd enjoy five rambunctious children. When I volunteered to take Eliazer and Rebekah, I could see Abigail relax a little. I knew I'd done the right thing.

Eliazer and Rebekah were full of stories. They even told the children stories about me as a child. I'm sure I'll be reminded of those for years to come. The rest of the day was full of laughter and love. And when evening came I was sorry to see it end.

But not long after we brought the animals in and dimmed the lights, there was a pounding on the door. Reuben pushed the ox out of the way and opened the door. Over his shoulder I saw Abigail, looking frantic, and a young man and woman.

"Please," said Abigail, "you'll have to help. We've no more room."

"Well, neither do we!" I thought to myself. But then I looked more closely at the couple. The man looked vaguely familiar. When I looked at the girl, I caught my breath. I'd been where she was — five times! I heard myself say, "Get them inside."

Where was I going to put them? I didn't know. But it was too cold for the girl to give birth outside. Could I move Eliazer and Rebekah out of the little guest room, so often used for birthing in the past? No, they were probably asleep by now. And they were too old to have anything but a comfortable bed.

Well, the front room it would have to be.

As the couple came inside, I looked more closely, "Joseph?"

Joseph was my second cousin and we'd played together as children.

He threw back his head and laughed. "Yes, it's me! And this is my wife, Miriam. We didn't plan to arrive until tomorrow, but when it seemed that the baby wouldn't wait, we pushed on."

I looked at the girl. I could see she was frightened, but still remarkably calm for one about to give birth for the first time. And among strangers, at that, with lots of livestock looking on!

I sent Reuben to get some extra straw and we improvised a bed for Miriam. Frankly, I was in my element. I'd done this five times myself and helped countless others.

Miriam looked strong and healthy and determined. I thought, this birth will probably go all right.

It did. There was all the usual sweat and blood and groaning. But when you hear that first cry, you know it was all worth it. Although the place was a little unusual, it was a birth just like most others.

What a beautiful baby boy they had! Yeshua, Joseph said his name was. A nice, strong, plain name. I liked that.

Then we improvised a bed for the baby in the feed trough. He was so well swaddled, the straw would never scratch him. I felt pleased and satisfied — and tired.

It was then that the odd things began to happen. First it was some shepherds. They came and just stared at the baby. Joseph and Miriam didn't seem very surprised. "Why did those shepherds come?" I asked.

"Well," said Joseph, "this is God's special child."

That didn't mean much. I thought all five of mine were God's special children, too.

As the shepherds left, I asked them why they'd come. "We saw lights and heard voices from the sky. They told us that the Messiah had been born and that we'd find him in Bethlehem, sleeping in a feeding trough."

It was very strange. I'd heard the Messiah might come from Bethlehem. But surely the Messiah wasn't Joseph's son. He and Miriam were just plain, simple working people like us.

We invited Joseph and Miriam to stay a few days, until she got her strength back enough to travel and felt comfortable with the baby. Eliazer and Rebekah tottered off down the road. We all breathed prayers that they'd get home safely.

Then the next strange thing happened. Some men arrived. They had heavy accents and the fabric of their robes was the very finest. They came with camels. The children went wild. They'd never seen camels before. I'd only seen them once or twice, and not close up. To tell the truth, I was kind of excited, too.

The men with accents also wanted to see the baby. They had fancy little boxes and they gave them to Joseph and Miriam.

I asked them, "Why did you want to see the baby? And how did you come here?"

"We're astrologers," they replied. "We saw signs in the heaven that told us the King of the Jews was being born. We've traveled many months to worship him."

The King of the Jews? He was a very nice baby, I had to agree, but still ... King of the Jews? Messiah? My second cousin's child?

I couldn't make sense of it all. But clearly something must be different about this baby.

Joseph and Miriam left. Instead of heading back to Nazareth, they headed for Egypt. Joseph said he'd had a dream that that was what he was supposed to do. He'd been a dreamy child. People don't change much, I guess.

We still had a few more guests, courtesy of the census. I didn't have much time to think then, but when things got back to normal, I did. Messiah? King? It seemed farfetched and I was skeptical.

Still — there were all those strange visitors. I supposed it could be true. And if it was, what an honor. The Messiah had been born under our roof!

Then I started to feel bad. What if I'd actually put the baby Messiah to bed in a feeding trough? Would God judge me for such an irreverent act?

Reuben just laughed at me. "Jochaved, if God's judged you, he's judged you worthy to help with the birth of the Messiah."

"No," I said, "that was just an accident. If Abigail had been more ... well, if she'd have been...."

I wanted to say that if she'd been more prepared, the baby would have been born at her house. But that made no sense. Abigail had been more prepared than me for the whole census!

After many years and five children, Reuben knew what I was thinking. "No, Jochaved. Abigail wasn't prepared. She spent weeks preparing her house. She cleaned and ground flour and made curtains. Her house was prepared, but she wasn't. But you ... you've spent your whole life preparing your heart!"

Hmmm ... well ... to think I'd envied Abigail her nice and tidy house. Maybe that wasn't as important as I'd thought. I'll have to think about that. Sometime ... but right now I smell the bread burning and here comes Eli with something in his hands.

Pamela J. Abbey

A Shepherd

Night Watch

Luke 2:8-15

It began as a night just like any other night. We spent the usual confused time separating our flocks into their own sheepfolds. And then each of us curled up in the gate to the fold to keep wild and hungry things from creeping in.

Someone sat by the fire, of course, so that it wouldn't go out. Others acted as lookouts around the edge of the area.

The night wasn't that cold, but since we were outdoors for all of it, it always seemed to be a numbing cold, even in the spring. The shepherds on lookout would tell stories to keep themselves alert. Those of us curled up in the gates would sleep uneasily, knowing that the tap on the shoulder would come soon enough for us to take our place on watch.

It was not a comfortable life. And there really was no hope of anything very different. We were men who lived on the edges of life. Shepherds lived in sight of the towns, just as we could see Bethlehem in the distance. But we were always out there on the edges of things, except for brief visits to the market. Sometimes we'd go to the Temple to take lambs that would be used for sacrifice.

But we weren't really part of the community. People looked down their noses at us. I guess they thought we were a necessary evil. Someone had to look after the flocks. Someone had to know how to birth the lambs. But it wasn't a job that took much wit or education. Certainly we didn't have much money, or own much of anything, for that matter.

And because we lived in the fields and followed the rhythms of the flocks and the weather, we couldn't keep the rituals of our faith. We seldom made sacrifices or went through the ritual cleansings. Most people considered us unclean, no matter how faithful we might be in our hearts. So we lived on the edge of our community's life.

I didn't think much about those things. It was just my life. And in many ways I liked my life. I enjoyed being outdoors, living in nature. I loved the camaraderie I had with the other shepherds. On good days, I even liked the sheep!

So — it had been an ordinary day. We were all hoping for an uneventful, ordinary night. We settled in. I'd drawn second watch, so I arranged myself in the gate, waiting for the tap on the shoulder in a few hours. Just as I drifted off to sleep, it happened. Or began to happen, maybe I should say. I guess it was the music, first, that roused me. It was so loud, it felt like it was filling me up. Yet I'm not sure that I even heard it with my ears. I seemed to hear it somewhere deep inside. It was the most incredible sound. I know I'll never hear anything like it again, at least not in this life.

Then there was the brightness. The moon was up that night, and it was nearly full, but it wasn't that. The whole sky began to glow. It seemed to shimmer and throb with light. That's when I got scared. Even an eclipse of the sun or moon shakes me up a little. This unknown brightness was frightening.

Then shapes began to appear in the sky. They seemed almost human, yet they were different in some way I can't describe. They were here and then there. You could see through them, as though they were ghosts. My fear changed to terror.

Then a voice came. Again, I don't know how I heard it, but it seemed to fill the sky. The voice said, "Fear not." And as petrified as I was, the voice was so strong and gentle, and the music so clear and vibrant, that I did stop being afraid. I got caught up in what was happening.

The voice went on. It told us there was good, joyful news. The voice said the Messiah, the Anointed One, had been born. He was in Bethlehem, the little town we could see in the distance. The voice said this baby, the Messiah, was wrapped up in cloths just like all babies are wrapped. And that he was lying in a manger, the feeding trough for livestock.

The music swelled. It sounded like a huge group of pilgrims singing, only much better. All I could do, all any of us could do, was to fall to the ground. We knew, somehow, we were in the presence of something divine.

The figures dimmed; the light faded. Gradually the music, too, drifted into the distance. Slowly we got up and looked at each other. There was no question that we would go as fast as we could into Bethlehem.

We forgot the sheep and ran into town. There, on the edge of town, we saw a small house with a stable snugged up against it. We heard a baby's cry coming from the stable and we knew the figures in the sky had been right. So we went in and bowed and worshiped.

Although we may not have gone to the Temple often, or prayed or washed or tithed like the good people, we knew the stories. We knew a Messiah would come some day, and that he would come from the city of David, Bethlehem. And here he was, mysteriously coming to us as a child.

Even more mysteriously, there we were worshiping him, shepherds who lived out on the edges of things. It all seemed very strange.

And then it hit me. Something even stranger! Where were the crowds? Why weren't hundreds of people pressed around the stable? Why had the paths been clear as we ran to town? The music, the light, the voice — it had all been overwhelming. We weren't that far from town. Surely everyone for miles had seen and heard it.

But it was just us — and the mother and the father and the animals and, of course, the baby Messiah.

We stayed a while, sitting in wonder and amazement. We left shortly before dawn. Slowly we made our way back out into the fields. I kept thinking, "Surely now that daylight's here, people will make their way to see." But there was no one on the roads except for an occasional traveler.

There were many wonders that night, but the one I have wondered about most is: "Why us?" Why were a bunch of shabby shepherds the first to see God's Messiah? We sure weren't much to look at. We didn't speak well. We didn't have a place of honor in the world — just the opposite, in fact. We weren't even faithful in the usual sense of the word. Why us?

One day as I was pondering these questions, it came to me. Maybe all those things were the very reasons that we could see and hear and others didn't! I don't know the scripture very well, but I do remember some words from one of the prophets. Isaiah, I think it was.

He was thinking about what the Messiah would be like and he wrote, "The Lord has anointed me; he has sent me to announce good news to the humble...."

So maybe instead of the way I had thought it would be, with the Messiah striding through the Temple and the halls of palaces, maybe God intended all along to start with people like us. Because there was no one much more humble than a shepherd. And if God intended to start with people like us, then that really was good news.

There we were living on the edge of town, on the edge of society, on the edge of religion. There wasn't much to distract us.

That was the other thing I thought of. Bethlehem was small but it was an awfully busy place, especially with that census thing going on. Whenever I went into town, I didn't like to stay long. It was too noisy and crowded for me. It made it hard to think straight. So maybe one of the reasons God came to us shepherds, is that out on the edge of things, we could see better. We could hear better.

That's what a shepherd's life is. We watch for signs of danger, for the sudden quieting of birds. We watch for patches of greener pasture. We cock our ears for the sounds of water and look for the glint of sun on a still pond. We watch the sheep for signs of impending birth — or death. By nature and training, we were people who watched.

And maybe, we were people who needed more than anyone else to hear the good news. Those who have ears, let them hear, the saying goes.

Most of all, I wonder what became of that baby. He'd be a man by now. I guess that night has helped me figure out that he won't be showing up where I used to think he would — in the Temple and in palaces and with powerful people. Not a Messiah who came as a baby and slept in a manger and had a bunch of shepherds as his first guests. I wonder what his life will be like. Would I know him if I saw him?

You know, I am a shepherd, but sometimes I feel like I need one, too. I hate to compare myself to a sheep, but sometimes I find

I've wandered off the path. Sometimes I feel thirsty inside. Sometimes I feel hungry for something more. I could use a good shepherd to set me right again.

Shepherds are looked down on. Yet the prophets must have understood the way I feel inside sometimes. Because they compared God to a shepherd. There's a place in Ezekiel that I've always remembered. "For the Lord God says: Now I myself shall take thought for my sheep and search for them. I shall bring them home to their own country. I shall shepherd them on the mountains of Israel and by her streams. I shall feed them on good grazing ground. There they will rest in good pasture. I myself shall tend my flock, and find them a place to rest, says the Lord God."

I guess you can tell why I like that passage. It's my job description! And I guess it must be God's job description. And maybe it's the job description of the baby Messiah that I saw. That's what we all long for — a good shepherd. And maybe that baby was he. What strange good news — a good shepherd who comes first to shepherds.

Who knows? As for me, I guess I'll just keep wondering. And watching.

Pamela J. Abbey

An Angel

Tidings

Luke 2:8-14

(Angel enters, humming or whistling "Angels We Have Heard On High." Stops center and begins to pull "equipment" from bag or backpack.)

Let's see ... I've got my eighteen loud hosannas. There's my portable harp. My wing wax is packed. And, last but not least, my halo.

(Puts on tinsel halo.)

This thing is really more trouble than it's worth. It's always slipping off at a bad moment or getting tarnished. But this will be my last trip for a long time, so I guess I won't have to worry about it so much in the future.

I'm tired of being an angel. I know ... you think it's a great life, just sitting around heaven all day being musical, but it's not like that at all. We're God's messengers, that's what we are. The Lord is always sending us off somewhere to deliver a message. And it's never any place exciting.

Well, there *was* the fiery furnace, if you mean *that* kind of exciting! That was a miserable trip. I couldn't get the smoky smell out of my wings for weeks!

It's a continual grind, this business of delivering God's messages. How would you like it if every time you started a conversation you had to begin with "Fear not!"? Here I come with messages of God's love, and every time it's the old "Be not afraid" routine. It ruins my interpersonal relationships, let me tell you. Not to mention what it does to my ego. I'm a perfectly nice creature — friendly, considerate, interesting. Honestly, you'd enjoy meeting me at a dinner party. There's absolutely no reason I should always have to introduce myself with "Fear not."

A while back, I got so fed up I went to the Lord for help. The suggestion I got there was that I disguise myself. So I tried that with Moses. Remember the burning bush? (*Indicates self, proudly*) "And the angel of the Lord appeared to him in a flame of fire out of the middle of a bush."

Took an awful lot of energy to pull that one off! And poor Moses still hid his face, he was so afraid. Then when he finally stopped being afraid, I couldn't get him to stop talking! I was afraid I'd wear out and blow my cover. Besides, it was extremely warm. So disguises only help a little bit.

But the Lord got another bright idea. Called me over to the throne one day and said, "Why don't you try visiting people in their dreams, while they're asleep, instead of when they're awake? People accept all kinds of things in their dreams."

So I do that sometimes. I just visited the dream of a guy named Joseph not too long ago. But it's really hard work and it requires split-second timing. If I try to get into people's dreams early in the night, or just before they get up in the morning, they're likely to wake up and there I am saying, "Fear not," again.

And in the deepest part of the night it can be very difficult to break into a dream. The things that can happen while you're in there ... whew! ... highly unpredictable! I never know when it's going to turn into a nightmare.

So I complain and I joke about it, and I say that I don't understand why I have these problems. But that's not really true. I do understand. It's in that line from your scripture, "The glory of the Lord shone round about them." People are afraid of God's glory and a little bit of it is always clinging to me. I couldn't get rid of it even if I wanted to. So I frighten people.

Isn't it funny how they're frightened by what loves them most? Because the glory of God isn't a thing. We describe it as a thing ... like fire, or smoke, or thunder ... but that's not it at all. The glory of God is the Lord's yearning for creation. The glory of God is what loves you and me.

If we describe it like fire or smoke or thunder, it's only because love also acts like those things. Love is hot and it brings light, so we call it fire. Love can fill every tiny, remote part of our being, so we call it smoke. And love proclaims itself boldly and without fear, so we call it thunder.

It *is* awesome. Even after all these millennia with the Lord, I've never quite gotten over the power of it. But it's really nothing to be afraid of. It's not even foreign to you. Your scripture says, "The whole world is filled with God's glory." It's already here, if only you'd see it. Every time you love somebody or he or she loves you, that's part of the glory. Every time you say, "I'm sorry," it's part of God's glory. Every time you laugh and every time you cry, you have some of God's glory.

Still, it seems to be so hard for people to see it. And then I show up with a little bit of glory clinging to me and they're afraid and we're off on the same conversation: "Fear not."

So I really do understand. But that doesn't make it any easier. I'm still exhausted and tired of it all. So I went to God one last time and said, "I've had it! I can't handle one more person rejecting me. I can't take any more burning bushes or fiery furnaces and I don't have enough stamina to crash dreams. What do you suggest I do about it?"

I couldn't believe I'd spoken to the Almighty that way!

But God was wonderful. The Lord said, "I can see you're tired and worn out. You shouldn't have to take my messages anymore. You need a rest. Just let me think about how to do it."

So I waited, but without much hope, because for the life of me I couldn't see a way out of the dilemma. The messages still have to be delivered, even if no one wants to listen.

But eventually the Lord called me back and said, "I've solved it. I've figured out how to give you a rest."

"Really?"

"Yes. I'll go."

I didn't know what to say. How could such a thing happen? If the little bit of glory that clings to me frightens people, what would happen if the Lord showed up? But God had the answer.

"I'll go like one of them. I'll be one of them. You've been talking to them about the glory and love of God and it hasn't gotten through. So I'll go and show them. Enough talk."

And I said, "But, God, it's dangerous down there! Don't you know that?"

And the Lord replied, "Yes, I know it. I know it even better than you. But maybe in order to stop being afraid of my glory, my people need to see that it isn't just fire and smoke and thunder. They need to see what I'm willing to risk for them. They need to see that the glory of God can be contained in a human life."

I didn't understand it. I still don't understand it. I don't know how it's happening exactly or what will happen because of it. But I know that it *is*. And that's my trip tonight. To take one last message. A very simple one: "God is here. God is with you. Emmanuel."

It's time for me to be off. I have to introduce myself to some shepherds in just a few minutes. My fellow angels who can see into the future tell me that this day will be called Christ-mas. If they're right, have a blessed one. Think of me in my peaceful retirement. (*Starts to exit, then turns back*)

Oh ... and fear not!

Pamela J. Abbey

Youth Sunday

Introduction

On Youth Sunday we are called to worship to praise and thank God for the blessings of youth as they lead the congregation in their service of worship.

As young people prepare to lead, how can we, pastors or worship leaders, help them to express their thoughts and feelings, needs and concerns, as relating to the biblical text?

1. Celebrate diversity.

Not all youth enjoy being in the public eye, whether they are shy or lacking in confidence. However, they willingly serve as ushers, greeters, or takers of the offering. Given their creativity, ask for volunteers to make posters and banners of Jesus' parables or things youth enjoy doing at church.

Some cannot gather for a rehearsal, yet young people feel more reverent if they are not nervous, and reading through the worship service together beforehand creates a more effective and spiritual atmosphere of worship for all.

In some churches conflicts may arise around Youth Sunday. In one church the youth began with a popular CD about the need for love to conquer hate. As the music played, they danced in the chancel, moving to the music and their feelings. An adult stood up and walked out. Then a senior girl explained the Youth Fellowship was not there to shock the congregation but to communicate. She talked passionately about the importance of being an individual. Another adult stood up and left the sanctuary. Then one of the boys came forward and told how he no longer believed in the God of his Sunday school. He found God when he walked in the woods. Someone else walked out (but not to the woods). Another boy talked about war and killing and our nation's involvement, and more people left. One youth with long hair stood up and prayed, "God, bless all

67

the men here with long hair, and all those with short hair, and all those with no hair, and help them love one another for Christ's sake. Amen."

After Youth Sunday, the minister held open meetings every other Sunday evening so the different generations could gather and attempt to talk with one another. The minister later learned that one of the distinguished and reserved grandmothers, when asked when she had last actually experienced communion, replied, "Youth Sunday!"

2. Pray for the youth of your congregation of faith, for prayer, as scripture, God's Word, is the path where there is none.

3. Provide a possible service of worship.

The following is a suggested service you may wish to change to fit your own group. It is based on Mark 4:34 as the scripture: "He [Jesus] did not speak to them except in parables...."

Youth Sunday

Service Of Worship

Youth Sunday

Call to Worship
God calls us through God's Word and story. Come, let us worship the Great Storyteller.

Or, "Your word, O Lord, is a lamp to our feet and a light to our path" (Psalm 119:105). Come, let us worship the Lord. Amen.

Processional Hymn "Tell Me The Stories Of Jesus"

Prayer of Confession
Dear Lord, forgive our wandering thoughts, our wayward ways, our weary words as we predict and plan and proclaim rather than patiently awaiting your guidance and presence. We are people who want to choose and control rather than love and be loved by your grace and mercy, through Christ Jesus. Amen.

Prayer of Assurance
Jesus said, "I know that and I love you."

Or, "The Lord is gracious and merciful, slow to anger and abounding in steadfast love. The Lord is good to all, and his compassion is over all that he has made" (Psalm 145:8-9).

Or, "You are forgiven. In Christ's name you are a new creature. Amen."

Affirmation of Faith
I believe in God, the Poet of Creation,

Through Jesus the Word, who died a parabler of God and rose to be the Parable of God,

And the Holy Spirit who enables us to hear God's Word and do it. Amen.

Children's Time

(Bring a stuffed toy of Winnie the Pooh)

How many of you know my friend, Winnie the Pooh? He asked me to tell you a story about him, because Pooh likes stories. I hope you do, too.

One morning Winnie the Pooh dropped in at Rabbit's hole in hopes of finding a Little Something, and he did, and he ate every bit of honey, condensed milk, and bread that was in Rabbit's hole. When there was nothing more to eat, Pooh said, "I must be going."

"Must you?" asked Rabbit.

"Well, I could stay a little longer if ... if I ..." Pooh thought there might be something more to eat.

Rabbit said, "As a matter of fact, I was just going out myself."

"Oh, good-bye then." Pooh started to climb out of the hole. He put his nose out, then he pulled with his front paws and pushed with his back paws and his ears came out and his shoulders and ... "Help, I'm stuck!" Pooh could not move.

Finding the front door full, Rabbit went out the back door. "Oh, Pooh, are you stuck?"

"No, just resting and thinking."

But when Rabbit offered his paw to help, Pooh took it. Rabbit pulled and pulled, and Pooh said, "Your door is too small."

Rabbit said, "No, it's from eating too much. I will get Christopher Robin."

When Christopher Robin arrived, he said, "Silly old Bear," and pulled and pulled. "We will have to wait for you to get thin again."

"How long?" asked Pooh.

"About a week."

Pooh began to sigh and then found he couldn't because he was so tightly stuck, and a tear rolled down his cheek, as he said, "Then would you read a Sustaining Book, such as would help and comfort a Wedged Bear in Great Tightness?" Christopher promised that he would.[1]

Talk Together

Why did Pooh get stuck in Rabbit's hole? What helped Pooh? What is your favorite story? Do you know anyone who told "sustaining stories"?

Prayer of Dismissal

"Dear God, thank you for the stories Jesus told that help us know your love. Amen."

Scripture Reading

Psalter Reading: Psalm 119:105
Old Testament. Jeremiah 1:4-10
Epistle: Romans 10:8-17
Gospel: Mark 4:30-34

Or, use a paraphrase of the text: "The kingdom of God is like a story, which when sown upon the soul, is the smallest of all the stories on earth, yet when it is warmed by wonder and watered with imagination, it grows up and becomes the meaning of Existence, and puts forth a World of Possibility so that the creatures of earth can make their homes in it."[2]

Sermon

Dialogue, drama, or discussion of the text are different forms of telling the parables of Jesus. Jesus said, "Heaven and earth will pass away, but my words will never pass away." He taught through his parable. He did not speak to them except in story.

[Assist the youth storyteller to tell one of Jesus' parables or a story that conveys the meaning of faith for the youth. Or use poetry.]

God, knowing our need for metaphor,
Enfleshed the Word so we could see.
As the sun penetrates the world with light,
May the Word with wisdom and wonder enter within,
For unto us a Word is born.

71

Hymn of Response   "I Love To Tell The Story"

Litany of Praise and Thanksgiving
Leader: As people who love to tell the story, we thank you, God,
          for the stories of Abraham and Sarah, Moses and Miriam,
          David, Ruth, Isaiah, Jeremiah, Peter, Mary, and Jesus.
All: **I love to tell the story.**
Leader: We thank you, God, for the stories of Jesus; how he made
          the blind see, the deaf hear, and the dumb speak.
All: **I love to tell the story.**
Leader: We thank you for the stories Jesus told about the shep-
          herd who lost one lamb.
All: **I love to tell the story.**
Leader: The story of the loving father who forgave his prodigal
          son and his prejudiced one.
All: **I love to tell the story.**
Leader: The story of the kingdom of God as small as a tiny seed
          and as large as a tree for nesting.
All: **I love to tell the story.**
Leader: We thank you, Lord, for our lives which are your stories.
All: **Amen.**

Offering
    Youth may play a musical instrument; sing one of the songs
from *Jesus Christ Superstar* or *Godspell* as a solo or with the choir;
or express love and praise to God through movement to music.

Doxology

Hymn of Commitment   "Thy Word Is A Lamp"

Prayers of the People and the Lord's Prayer
    Most gracious loving God, open our ears so we may hear your
word in the sound of the birds and the angels singing, our eyes to
see the majesty of the stars and moon and feel the power of the
psalmists' songs of praise, our noses to smell the odors of sanctity
and of the sea and the rain-soaked rose. Fill us with your Spirit so

we may share in the Good News of your gospel and send out your word to accomplish your will. Watch over the words of our mouth and the meditations of our heart so they may be accceptable in your sight, our Lord and Redeemer. Amen.

Our Father, who art in heaven ...

Benediction

Go now into the world in the name of God, the Word-Maker, through Jesus Christ, God's Word, and the Holy Spirit who enables us to hear and do that word. Amen.

Elaine M. Ward

---

1. A. A. Milne, *The House At Pooh Corner* (New York: Puffin Books, 1992).

2. Elaine M. Ward, *Love in a Lunchbox: Poems and Parables for Children's Worship* (Nashville, Tennessee: Abingdon Press, 1996), p. 7. Used by permission.

Contributors

Stan Purdum is the pastor of Centenary United Methodist Church in Waynesburg, Ohio. He is also the editor of the preaching journal *Emphasis*, and has written extensively for both the religious and secular press. Purdum is the author of *Roll Around Heaven All Day* and *Playing In Traffic*, both accounts of his long-distance bicycle journeys, as well as *New Mercies I See* (CSS), a collection of parish stories revealing God's grace.

Pamela J. Abbey is a United Methodist minister whose early working years were spent in professional theater. She is currently the pastor of Concord United Methodist Church in Concord, California, and has previously served three other congregations in northern California. Abbey holds degrees in theater from the University of Indianapolis (B.A.) and the University of Minnesota (M.A.) as well as an M.Div. degree from Pacific School of Religion in Berkeley, California.

Elaine M. Ward is a storyteller/writer/preacher who served for nearly twenty years as Minister of Children at University Park United Methodist Church in Dallas, Texas. She is a graduate of Capital University, Union Theological Seminary (New York City), and Lancaster Theological Seminary, where she was writer-in-residence for seven years. Now a resident of Austin, Texas, Ward is the author of *Asking For Wonder, And The Sea Lay Down, Alleluia!* and *Story Time At The Altar* (CSS), as well as *Love In A Lunchbox: Poems And Parables For Children's Worship* (Abingdon).